Mystery at the Mill

Elspeth Rawstron

About this Book

For the Student

🎧   Listen to the story and do some activities on your Audio CD

🗩   Talk about the story

ban°   When you see the blue dot you can check the word in the glossary

P   Prepare for Cambridge English: Preliminary (PET) for Schools

For the Teacher

 A state-of-the-art interactive learning environment with 1000s of free online self-correcting activities for your chosen readers.

Go to our Readers Resource site for information on using readers and downloadable Resource Sheets, photocopiable Worksheets and Answer Keys. Plus free sample tracks from the story.

www.helblingreaders.com
For lots of great ideas on using Graded Readers consult Reading Matters, the Teacher's Guide to using Helbling Readers.

Level 5 Structures

Modal verb *would*	Non-defining relative clauses
I'd love to ...	Present perfect continuous
Future continuous	*Used to / would*
Present perfect future	*Used to / used to doing*
Reported speech / verbs / questions	Second conditional
Past perfect	Expressing wishes and regrets
Defining relative clauses	

Structures from other levels are also included.

Helbling Readers e-zone is the brand new state-of-the-art easy-to-use interactive learning environment from Helbling Languages. Each book has its own set of online interactive self-correcting cyber homework activities containing a range of reading comprehension, vocabulary, listening comprehension, grammar and exam preparation exercises.

Students test their language skills in a stimulating interactive environment. All activities can be attempted as many times as necessary and full results and feedback are given as soon as the deadline has been reached. Single student access is also available.

Teachers register free of charge to set up classes and assign individual and class homework sets. Results are provided automatically once the deadline has been reached and detailed reports on performance are available at a click.

1000s of free online interactive activities now available.

www.helbling-ezone.com

Contents

Meet the Author

Hello Elspeth, tell us a little about yourself.
I studied drama at university and then worked for a theatre newspaper in London. Later, I decided to train as an English teacher. By a strange twist of fate•, I found a teaching job in Istanbul in Turkey and I have lived and worked there ever since.

Where do you get your ideas for stories?
The idea for a story often comes when I visit a place. I feel that I'd like to read a story set in that place.

Why did you choose Salts Mill as the location for the story?
Some places make a big impression• on you and Salts Mill is one of those places. It used to be a huge• old textile mill• but now it's an art gallery. The history of the mill and its owner is fascinating. It's the perfect place for a mystery story.

What is the main theme of the story?
The main theme of the story is children working long hours and in difficult conditions. The characters in the book are fictional but in the past a lot of very young girls like Emily and Grace worked in mills like Salts Mill and a lot of the girls died young. Around the world today, children are still working in dangerous conditions and dying young.

I would like to thank Roger Clarke, an author and local historian•, for helping me with my research into the historical background• of the mill and my mum for taking me there in the first place.

Glossary
- **background:** things that happened at the time of the story
- **historian:** person who studies history
- **huge:** very big
- **make a big impression:** have a big effect
- **textile mill:** building with machinery for making a type of fabric (e.g. wool)
- **twist of fate:** unplanned event

Before Reading

1 At the heart of the story, there is a mystery at a mill. Look at the pictures in the book. Make predictions about the story.

a) What do you think happens? Tick (✔).
☐ death ☐ theft ☐ murder ☐ war
☐ kidnapping ☐ romance ☐ ghosts ☐ business

b) When does the story take place? Tick (✔).
☐ in the past ☐ in the present
☐ in the past and the present ☐ in the future

2 There are two stories within the story. Answer the questions using the pictures in the book to help you guess.

a) Which story has the happiest ending? The story in the past or the story in the present?

b) How does the story in the past end? With a death or with marriage and children?

c) How does the story in the present end? With a dream coming true or with a death?

3 Look at the pictures in the book and write the characters' names next to the sentences.

a) She works in a mill. ....
b) She goes to school. ....
c) She investigates a mystery in the snow. ....
d) She suffers in the cold but is very courageous. ....
e) She gets into trouble in a shop. ....
f) She has two friends who manage to help her. ....

Before Reading

1 Part of the story takes place at Salts Mill. Read and complete the text with the words below. Then listen and check your answers.

| polluted | cheaper | better | local | huge | educational |
| terrible | great | healthier | Industrial |

Salts Mill

At the time of the **(a)** .... Revolution, Bradford was a very **(b)** .... city. People lived in **(c)** .... conditions and many died young. A mill owner, Sir Titus Salt wanted his workers to live in **(d)** .... conditions and have a **(e)** .... life, so he built a mill outside the city. It was completed in 1853 and it was called Salts Mill. Sir Titus Salt also built a village with houses for his workers to live in, shops, a church and a park. He later built two schools and a social club and an **(f)** .... institute for adults.

The mill continued to produce cloth for another century. In 1976 it was still producing £4 million of cloth a year. At the end of the seventies, a lot of **(g)** .... foreign cloth was imported into Britain. Many mills in England lost all their business and had to close. Salts Mill closed in 1986.

In 1987, a 37-year old **(h)** .... businessman bought the mill and opened an art gallery, which houses the largest collection of the Bradford-born artist, David Hockney's paintings. There is also a **(i)** .... bookshop, an art shop, an interior design shop and a restaurant. Anyone who loves art, books, food or history will fall in love with the mill. It's **(j)** .... !

2 **Is there a factory, mill or coal mine near where you live? Find out about its history and write a paragraph.**

3 **Part of the story takes place by a canal. Label the photos of the canal with the words below.**

> barge   canal   towpath   lock   canal bank

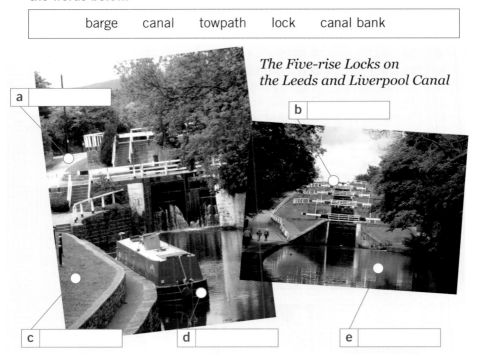

The Five-rise Locks on the Leeds and Liverpool Canal

a

b

c

d

e

4 **Use the words from Exercise 3 to complete these sentences from the story.**

   a) Then sometimes, my friend Grace and I went for a walk down by
      the ....

   b) We were sitting on the grassy .... when a canal
      .... went by.

   c) It was hard pedalling along the snowy .... by the side
      of the canal but Jake was determined.

   d) Water poured down on them, but the barge didn't sink, and then
      it clicked. 'It's OK. We're in a .... ,' she thought.

Before Reading

1 These verbs are from the story. Match them to their definitions.

a) ☐ to grip	**1** to talk very quietly
b) ☐ to grab	**2** to sew two things together
c) ☐ to squeal	**3** to look at for a long time
d) ☐ to stitch	**4** to talk
e) ☐ to stare	**5** to hold tightly
f) ☐ to mumble	**6** to cry out
g) ☐ to chat	**7** to take quickly
h) ☐ to slam	**8** to shut with force

2 Match these nouns from the story with the pictures.

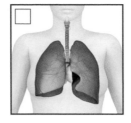

a) wool	**b)** lungs	**c)** leaflets
d) roll of cloth	**e)** leather book	**f)** cart

3 Use the words from Exercise 2 to answer these questions.

a) Which thing do you think Caterina finds in her grandmother's attic?

....

b) Which thing do you think Emily finds by the canal?

....

4 One of the characters, Uncle Sanjit, is a clothes designer who opens a shop. He designs and then produces his own clothes. What do you know about the production of clothes? Put the different processes of clothes production in order. Write the process under the correct picture.

> Selling the clothes.   Designing the clothes.
>
> Making the clothes.   Choosing the material to make the clothes.

a) ....

....

b) ....

....

c) ....

....

d) ....

....

5 Do you like buying clothes? In groups of three discuss what type of clothes you buy and where you buy them from.

6 Where are most of your clothes made? Look at the labels and find out. Do a survey in class and report back to your teacher.

The Diary

The year was 1859. Charles Darwin's *On the Origins of Species* was published. Big Ben started ticking° at the Houses of Parliament in London. Charles Dickens, the famous English writer, published *A Tale of Two Cities*. The Industrial Revolution had by now changed the face of England and my great-great grandmother started working at Salts Mill, a woollen mill° in Bradford. She was only eight years old.

> The air was full of a fine white dust° that almost choked me°. The sound of the machines was deafening°. I didn't know whether to cover my eyes or my ears with my hands. I wanted to turn and run but strong hands pushed me into the room. I wanted to scream but no one would hear me…
> I never forgot my first day at Salts Mill.
> Emily

The year was 2012 and Caterina was sitting at a table in a corner of the school canteen°. It was lunchtime and she could hear the chatter° and clatter° of plates and knives and forks.

Jake had finished his lunch and he was just about to leave the canteen when he saw her. Her long red hair was pulled back into a pony tail. He couldn't see her eyes but he knew that they were green. She was reading something. Maybe it was the leaflet° that everybody was talking about. He had to talk to her about it and now was probably a good time.

Glossary

- **canteen:** restaurant in a school or workplace
- **chatter:** noise of people talking
- **choked me:** made breathing difficult
- **clatter:** noise of objects touching
- **deafening:** very loud
- **dust:** small particles
- **leaflet:** printed sheet of paper giving information
- **ticking:** sound a clock makes every second
- **woollen mill:** building with machinery for making wool

13

Caterina was reading the first paragraphs of the leaflet again when a shadow fell across the table and she heard the chair opposite being pulled out from under the table. Then she looked up and saw Jake. He was tall with dark brown hair and dark brown eyes. Most people said that he was good-looking. He had a nice smile, but right now he wasn't smiling.

'Caterina, what you're doing is unfair•,' he said. 'That's my Uncle Sanjit's shop. He's worked hard for years to save the money to open that shop,' he continued.

'Well then, he should be more careful about what he sells in it. The children who make those clothes are younger than you and me,' said Caterina defiantly•, her green eyes flashing.

'It's that visit to Salts Mill last month that has upset you•, isn't it?' said Jake. 'That's OK. We all found it quite upsetting•,' he continued.

Upsetting
What has upset you recently?

'No... well, in a way, yes. It's supposed to be history – the workhouses• and the child labour. But it isn't history, is it? Who made that scarf you're wearing? How much did you pay for it?'

'A fiver•,' Jake replied proudly.

'Have you ever asked yourself why it was so cheap?'

'No. And your point is?'

'My point is that some child on the other side of the world is having a horrible life so that you can wear trendy• clothes,' said Caterina, upset.

Glossary

- **a fiver:** five pounds
- **defiantly:** openly disagreeing with; going against
- **trendy:** fashionable
- **unfair:** not right
- **upset you:** made you sad
- **upsetting:** disturbing
- **workhouses:** places where poor people received food and a bed in return for work

'I don't care who made my scarf. All I'm asking is that you don't stand outside my uncle's shop handing out* leaflets,' said Jake.

'It's too late to stop,' said Caterina. 'The leaflets are printed.'

'But this isn't about a sweatshop* in Asia. It's about Bradford. And it's not even about Bradford today. It's about Bradford nearly two centuries ago,' said Jake, surprised.

'The first page is about the past but the other pages are about children's lives today,' said Caterina.

'What is this?' asked Jake pointing to the first paragraph. 'It looks like an extract from a diary or maybe a letter.'

'Not exactly,' said Caterina. 'Emily couldn't read or write. She never went to school.' Caterina took an old leather book from her bag and passed it to Jake. 'My grandmother died last week,' she added.

'Oh, I didn't know. I'm sorry,' mumbled* Jake.

'Well, she did and I found this in her attic.'

'So who's Emily?' asked Jake. 'She can't be your grandmother. Your grandmother wasn't alive in 1859.'

'No, Emily was my great-great grandmother*,' said Caterina. 'She told my grandmother her life story. Then my grandmother wrote it down for her in this little book. That's where I got the extract from for the leaflet. You can read it if you like. It's very interesting.'

'Maybe another time,' said Jake, closing the small leather book and pushing it back across the table towards Caterina. 'I've got basketball practice now.'

Caterina waited for him to get up but he didn't. He was studying her face. 'All the girls fancy* him,' she thought, 'but not me. I've got more important things to think about.'

- **fancy:** like in a special way
- **great-great grandmother:** her grandmother's grandmother
- **handing out:** giving people
- **mumbled:** said quietly and unclearly
- **sweatshop:** place employing workers for long hours in poor conditions

Then Jake frowned°. 'You're really serious about all this, aren't you?'

'Yes,' said Caterina. 'Yes, I'm really serious about all this.'

'My uncle's not going to like it if you ruin° his business.'

'Yeah, well. Those girls in Asia are not too happy about working seventy hours a week for peanuts° to support your uncle's rotten° business,' Caterina replied.

Jake was still staring at her and the book was still on the table between them. Caterina could sense° people were watching and talking about them. Well, there was nothing to look at or talk about. There was nothing between her and Jake and there never would be.

Jake stood up.

'I'll see you around°,' he said. Then he was gone. Caterina watched him walk across the room and disappear.

The empty places at her table were soon filled by inquisitive° girls. 'What did Jake want?' 'Did he ask you out?'

'Of course not,' said Caterina indignantly° and she pushed the leather book into her bag. She didn't want to show it to anyone else just now. And she certainly didn't know why she had shown it to Jake. 'Of course he wasn't interested in it. How stupid of me to show it to him!' she thought.

'What did he want then?' the girls persisted.

'If you must know,' said Caterina, 'he asked me not to stand outside his uncle's shop on Saturday.'

'And are you still going to?' asked Helena. Everybody knew about her protest on Saturday.

'Of course I'm still going to,' said Caterina and she picked up her bag and walked out of the room.

Glossary

- **frowned:** made an unhappy facial expression
- **indignantly:** a little angrily
- **inquisitive:** curious
- **peanuts:** (here) very little money
- **rotten:** terrible
- **ruin:** destroy
- **see you around:** maybe I'll see you sometime in the future by chance
- **sense:** feel

Cheap Scarves

Jake threw the ball but he missed the basketball hoop•. He couldn't stop thinking about the extract he had read in the leaflet about Emily. Now he wanted to read the rest of Emily's story in the leather book; but he couldn't tell Caterina that, could he? He had never thought about Bradford's past before or how it was connected with the present. It was strange how history repeated and repeated itself. It was strange how events in one country at one point in time could happen in another country at a later point in time. Were no lessons ever learnt?

'Hey, Jake, you missed my pass,' said Simon, slapping• Jake on the back and dragging• his thoughts back to the game. 'What's up•?'

'Nothing,' said Jake. 'Look, I'm sorry. I have to go.'

'Don't tell me. It's that girl in the canteen, isn't it? Have you got a crush on• her or something?'

'No, of course not. It's just there's something I've got to do.'

'Can't it wait till after the game?'

'No, it can't.' And with that Jake left the sports hall. He heard his team mates shouting at him to stay, but he ignored them. They had a right to be angry, he knew. The team had an important match on Sunday and they needed to train hard. But, he couldn't concentrate on the game; so right now he wasn't any use to them. He looked at his watch. It was still lunchtime. 'Caterina might still be in the canteen,' he thought and he ran over there straight away. It was late and there weren't many students left in the canteen. But Caterina was still there looking through the leather book.

Glossary

- **dragging:** bringing with force
- **have a crush on:** like in a romantic way
- **hoop:** circle for scoring points in basketball
- **slapping:** hitting
- **What's up?:** What's the problem?

18

'Thank goodness, you're still here,' said Jake as he walked over to Caterina.

'What do you want now, Jake?' said Caterina.

'The thing is, I was thinking about your leaflet and I'd really like to read it,' said Jake, quickly.

'Are you serious?' said Caterina.

'Totally! I've been thinking about what you said and I'd like to know more.' He paused. 'My grandfather came here from India to work in one of the factories in the 1950s. Conditions were very different from your great-great grandmother's time but I'm sure they were still hard.'

'Yes, but at least he was an adult,' said Caterina. 'Here, read this and you won't want to buy any more cheap scarves!' Caterina gave Jake her leaflet and this time he sat down and read it.

Yes, it's a great T-shirt but do you know the answers to these questions?
Where was the cotton picked to make the T-shirt?
And more importantly, who picked the cotton?
It doesn't tell you on the label, does it? But I can tell you.

Child labour is not a thing of the past. Millions of children around the world, from Egypt to India, from Pakistan to Mexico are working long hours to make the clothes you wear.

My name's Aziz and I live in Uzbekistan. Uzbekistan is one of the largest exporters of cotton in the world. Every autumn the schools in my town are shut down and all the students go with their teachers to work in the cotton fields. About a million children, between the ages of five and fourteen, work in the cotton fields. Last year I was sent to a cotton farm far from my home. I stayed in a room with no windows or electricity. We were paid 3 or 4 cents per kilo of cotton. Is it still such a great T-shirt?

My name's Anika.
I'm twelve years old and I live in Bangladesh.
My father and mother both work in a clothes factory.
They don't earn very much so they can't afford to send me to school.
My sister and I have to work in the factory, too. My sister is only nine years old.
Maybe I made the hooded top you're wearing while you were out enjoying yourself with your friends.

That baseball cap looks good, but do you know how many hours I spent sewing caps last year? My name is Parimeeta and I'm twelve years old.
I live in Delhi in India.
My grandmother was sick and she desperately needed money for medicine so she sent me to work. I went to school before but now I work 12 hours a day.

'OK, you win. I don't want to buy any more cheap scarves, but I still don't want you to stand outside my uncle's shop on Saturday,' said Jake. Then he remembered the book. He really wanted to read it but would Caterina still let him?

'You know earlier you said I could read your grandmother's book,' said Jake cautiously•.

'Yes,' said Caterina. 'And?'

'Well, can I?'

'Sure,' said Caterina and she smiled. Then she pulled the little leather book from her bag and gave it to Jake.

As soon as Jake got home that evening, he ran up to his room and took out the little leather book.

As you now know, my name's Emily, and this is my story.

My mother and father grew up in a weaver•'s village, a few miles outside Bradford, a mill town in the North of England. After my parents got married, they came to Bradford to look for work.

By this time, the Industrial Revolution was in full swing•. Bradford was the wool capital of the world, but living conditions were terrible. Often six people lived in one very small room. Black smoke poured from• the huge mill chimneys polluting the air. The river was polluted, so there was no clean drinking water. There were frequent outbreaks• of typhoid and cholera• and life expectancy• was very low. Many children died. In fact thirty percent of mill workers' children were dead by the age of fifteen.

Glossary

- **cautiously:** in a careful way
- **in full swing:** at the height of activity
- **life expectancy:** years expected to live
- **outbreaks:** sudden occurrences of disease
- **poured from:** came out quickly and in great quantities
- **typhoid and cholera:** fatal illnesses
- **weaver:** person who made fabric or baskets by hand

Industry

Is your town an industrial town?
Was it an industrial town in the past?
What did it produce?

Emily

My parents were lucky. In 1853, they found work at the new steam-powered° woollen mill a few miles outside Bradford. The owner, Titus Salt, wanted his workers to have better living conditions, so he built a whole village around his mill. At first, my parents took the train to work, but later they were given a house in the village of Saltaire, and that's where I spent my teenage years.

Family

Do you know what your grandparents did?

What about your great-grandparents?

Where did they live?

Find out and share in class.

My father was an overlooker°, so our house was bigger than the others. We had a living room, a kitchen and three bedrooms. We even had our own outside lavatory° and a small garden. The village was surrounded by countryside and it was a short walk from the house to a canal. We were lucky.

So now you know where I lived and worked, let's skip° a few years.

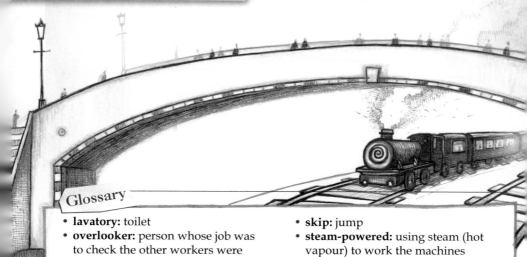

Glossary

- **lavatory:** toilet
- **overlooker:** person whose job was to check the other workers were working well
- **skip:** jump
- **steam-powered:** using steam (hot vapour) to work the machines

24

The year was 1869. Leo Tolstoy, the famous Russian author, wrote *War and Peace* , the vacuum cleaner• was invented and the Suez Canal was opened; and I was eighteen years old. The dust from the mill got into my lungs• and I had difficulty breathing but so did all my friends. That is, my friends who were still alive – the lucky ones. Lucy died last year. She was sixteen. Katy died the year before that. She was just fourteen. So you see, I was lucky.

But life wasn't all bad. We had fun, too. On Sundays we didn't work. There was the occasional visit to Brown & Muff, the department store in Bradford. Of course we didn't buy anything. We just stared at the magical window displays• of ladies' clothes. Clothes we made the cloth• for. Clothes we couldn't afford to wear. Then sometimes, my friend Grace and I went for a walk down by the canal.

And it was one cold but sunny Sunday in December, when we overheard• the conversation that changed our lives.

We were sitting on the grassy canal bank when a canal barge• went by. We could see the barge but nobody on the barge could see us. There was nothing unusual about the two men steering• the barge. What was unusual was that the barge stopped.

'This is the place, Harry,' said the tall man with the red hair.

'Are you sure about this?' asked his friend.

'Yes, there's an old cart• in the field over there. We can leave it under that until we come back tonight.'

They carried a heavy-looking object, wrapped• in some old sacks, off the barge.

Glossary

- **barge:** long, flat boat
- **cart:** open vehicle with wheels
- **cloth:** material for clothes
- **lungs:** organs used for breathing
- **overheard:** heard by chance
- **steering:** directing the course of
- **vacuum cleaner:** floor cleaner
- **window displays:** things in a shop window
- **wrapped:** covered

'What do you think it is?' whispered Grace and she gripped• my arm tightly.

'It looks like a dead body,' I said and she squealed•.

The men stopped.

'What was that?' asked the man called Harry.

'I don't know,' said the red-haired man. 'Maybe there's somebody up there behind those bushes•. I think we should go and take a look.' Grace went white and we stared at each other in terror. Then a cat leapt• out from under a bush and ran towards the men.

'Hey, Harry, it's nothing to worry about. It's just a cat. Let's get on with• the job•.'

'Jake, dinner time,' his mum called up the stairs.

'OK,' Jake shouted back. Bother•! The story had just started to get interesting and he wanted to carry on• reading. Why did meals always have to be at the most inconvenient times?

When Jake walked into the dining room, everybody was sitting round the table. They all stopped talking when he walked in. 'Oh, no! What have I done now?' he thought.

Then he saw his uncle.

Interesting

Why has Emily's story started to get interesting?

Are you sometimes interrupted while you are reading an interesting story?

What makes a story interesting?

- **bother:** (here) oh, no
- **bushes:** small trees
- **carry on:** continue
- **get on with:** finish

- **gripped:** held with force
- **job:** (here) what they have come to do
- **leapt:** jumped
- **squealed:** cried out

Jake

'Sit down, Jake,' said his father. 'We'll eat dinner first and then your uncle has something he wants to talk to you about.'

After dinner, his brother and sister went to do the washing up. Uncle Sanjit pulled a leaflet out of his pocket and put it on the table.

Jake's heart sank*. It was Caterina's leaflet.

'It's nothing to do with me,' said Jake.

'I know,' said his uncle, 'but I want you to stop this protest on Saturday. Can you talk to the girl? She's at your school, isn't she?'

'Yes and I've already tried to stop her but she won't listen to me.'

'Maybe you could just try and talk to her one more time. You know how much this shop means to me,' said Uncle Sanjit. 'These children in the leaflet – they haven't made the clothes in my shop.'

'How do you know that?' asked Jake.

'Because all the clothes in my shop are produced here in Bradford. The business is run by an old friend of mine. And I know every one of the people who stitch* my clothes and I can assure you that not one of them is younger than you.'

'And where did you get the material from?' asked Jake.

'From a respectable supplier* in London,' replied his uncle.

'And where was the cotton for that material picked?'

Now his uncle looked unsure of himself. 'I don't know, Jake.' There was another pause. 'Look, if it's really important to you, I'll ask the suppliers. They're coming up from London this evening.'

'Cool,' said Jake. 'Then I'll ask Caterina to call off* the protest, but I can't promise anything.'

Glossary

- **call off:** stop
- **heart sank:** suddenly became sad
- **stitch:** sew; make clothes

- **supplier:** provider; someone who makes the products available

'Thanks, Jake,' said Uncle Sanjit and he got up to leave. Then he sat down again. 'On second thoughts, why don't you call Caterina now? I don't want to leave anything to chance. I've waited a long time to open this shop.'

'I'm not sure if she'll come, Uncle,' mumbled Jake.

'Well, call and find out,' said Uncle Sanjit. 'Come on. Jump to it*. We haven't got all night.'

Jake took out his phone and texted Caterina.

My uncle's here now. Come and meet him. He'll explain everything.

Fab*. What's your address?

2 Princess Street ☺

Contact

How do you normally contact your friends?

Texts/Twitter/Facebook/phone/email/letter?

Caterina already knew the address but she didn't want Jake to know that. Quickly, she turned off her laptop and grabbed* her coat.

'I'm going to Samira's*,' she called to her mum.

'Don't be late,' her mum called back as the door slammed shut*.

- **fab**: great
- **grabbed**: quickly took
- **jump to it**: do it immediately
- **Samira's**: her friend Samira's house
- **slammed shut**: shut noisily and with force

Uncle Sanjit

It was only when Caterina stood on the doorstep that she began to feel nervous. Nervous about what? About confronting Jake's uncle or about seeing Jake? About confronting Jake's uncle, of course. No, that wasn't true. Caterina was never afraid of confrontation. In fact she loved it. The truth was, she was nervous about seeing Jake.

She pressed her finger on the doorbell – 5, 4, 3, 2 – the door opened and there was Jake.

'That was quick,' he said.

'Yeah, well I only live two streets away,' Caterina replied.

'Really? I never knew that,' said Jake. But Jake did. He knew a lot about her and he knew where she lived. He just didn't want Caterina to know that.

'Are we going to stand here all night or are you going to invite me in?' asked Caterina.

Jake smiled and stood aside*. 'Don't be too hard on him,' he said quietly so only she could hear. 'He's alright, my uncle.'

Jake's uncle was sitting at one end of a long dining table with a pile* of Caterina's leaflets in front of him.

'Uncle, this is Caterina. Caterina, this is my uncle Sanjit.'

'Sit down,' said Uncle Sanjit. 'You know, if you weren't trying to close me down, I'd employ you! You've got real talent,' he said.

'You're making money out of children,' said Caterina.

'You don't know that,' said Uncle Sanjit calmly. 'Hear me out* first. Don't jump to conclusions.' Then he explained everything about the business, just as he had explained to Jake.

'So,' said Caterina triumphantly, 'you don't know if children are employed in the production of your clothes or not. Did you read this?' she asked, pointing to the passage in her leaflet about cotton picking in Uzbekistan. 'The government of Uzbekistan said, "Children are not allowed to pick cotton in this country." But *Newsnight** filmed a field full of children picking cotton. One boy told *Newsnight*, "I won't go to school until November. I pick seventy kilos of cotton here a day." Another boy said, "I'm paid two pence a kilo." Some of the children were as young as nine. Cotton…'

'Yes, I see your point,' interrupted Uncle Sanjit, 'and I agree with you. Child labour is a terrible thing. I'll talk to my suppliers about it this evening. I promise. Now Caterina, tell me. What do you want to do when you leave school?'

'Me?' asked Caterina. 'I want to go to the London School of Economics. I'm going to study politics and then I'm going to be a politician and stop things like this from happening.'

Glossary

- **hear me out:** listen to what I have to say
- **Newsnight:** UK news programme
- **pile:** lots of, one on top of the other
- **stood aside:** moved to the side; allowed her to pass

'I see,' said Uncle Sanjit. 'You've got big dreams and I hope one day they'll come true for you. "Aim high•," my father always used to say. "You don't want to end up• like me working in a mill all your life." And he was right. I didn't. I wanted to open a shop and sell good quality clothes at affordable• prices. I wanted to employ my friends and most importantly of all, I wanted to design the clothes myself.'

'And did you design the clothes?' asked Caterina.

'Yes, I did,' replied Uncle Sanjit. 'And I hope you'll come to the shop on Saturday and see them. And maybe even like them. You see, Caterina. This shop was my dream. And I'm so close• to realizing it,' he said. 'Don't stop me now.'

Big Dreams

What do you want to do when you leave school?

Discuss with a partner and then tell the class.

'I won't stop you if your suppliers can guarantee that their cotton comes from a good source•,' said Caterina.

Glossary

- **affordable:** that people can buy
- **aim high:** (here) try and go for the best you can
- **end up:** finish

- **so close:** near
- **source:** place, person or thing from which something originates

'Yes,' said Uncle Sanjit. 'Well, that will be the first thing that I ask them then.' Then he looked at his watch. 'I have to go. The suppliers will be arriving at the station in twenty minutes.'

'Are you going to take them to the shop?' asked Caterina.

'Yes, we'll have the meeting in the shop. They're staying in the flat above the shop tonight.'

'Well, good luck then,' said Caterina. And in that second, she knew that she wanted to go to the shop, too. She needed to be at that meeting. She needed to hear what the suppliers said herself. She pushed her chair back and stood up.

'I have to go,' she said to Jake.

'Stay if you want,' he said.

'No, I have to go. I promised I wouldn't be late.'

'OK. See you at school tomorrow then,' he said trying not to look disappointed.

'Yeah, see you at school,' said Caterina.

Uncle Sanjit and Caterina left the house together.

'I'll give you a lift home* in the car, if you like.' said Uncle Sanjit.

'No, it's OK. I'll walk. I live just round the corner,' replied Caterina.

And so they went their separate ways. Each of them was thinking about the meeting with the suppliers. Each of them was thinking about children working long hours in factories and about cotton fields in faraway countries. Why is it that some children, who should be enjoying their youth and preparing for their futures, are denied* the dreams of Caterina and Uncle Sanjit?

<Glossary

• **denied:** (here) prevented from having   • **give you a lift home:** take you home

The Package

The door closed behind Caterina and Uncle Sanjit. It was seven
o'clock – too late to go and train with the basketball team now.
Besides, it had just started to snow. Then Jake remembered the book.
He went up the stairs two at a time and threw himself onto the bed.
He picked up the little leather book and carefully turned the pages
until he came to the right place in the story.

'Hey, Harry, it's nothing to worry about. It's just a cat. Let's get on
with the job.'

Then the two men walked across the field towards the old cart,
carrying the long body-shaped package•. Grace and I watched them
place• the package under the cart and then we watched them walk
away.

• **body-shaped package:** covered   • **place:** put
  object, shaped like a human body

'Let's go and see what's in the package,' I said, and stood up. My friend, Grace, pulled me down again.

'Are you mad?' she whispered loudly in my ear. 'Wait until we're *sure* they've gone. Look, I think I recognize one of the men.'

'Which one?' I asked.

'The tall man with the red hair. He works with my father. They load• the bales• of cloth onto the barges,' said Grace.

'Maybe that's not *all* they load onto the barges,' I said.

'What do you mean?' asked Grace.

'Dead bodies,' I said.

'Don't be silly,' said Grace and she shivered•. 'You're scaring me.'

Their voices drifted• across the field towards us and we caught some of their conversation. ' … here tonight … will pay us two shillings•.'

'They're coming again tonight,' I whispered excitedly. Then we watched the two men walk up through the field and climb over the wall at the top.

'Come on. They've gone now. Let's go and see what it is,' I said and held my hand out to Grace. Grace took my hand and I pulled her to her feet.

'I'll race you there,' I said and I ran off.

'Don't run,' said Grace. 'You know what happens when you run.'

I knew. But I didn't stop running. The sun was shining and there was a mystery to be solved. I didn't want to think about my illness that day. I got to the old cart and there was the package. I wanted to pull the old sacks off the package but something stopped me. I sat and waited for Grace.

Glossary

- **bales:** large amount of something fixed together
- **drifted:** came slowly through the air
- **load:** (here) put
- **shillings:** old units of British money
- **shivered:** shook a little with fear and cold

'Come on slow coach•! Hurry up!' I called excitedly.

Grace walked over to the cart and kneeled down beside me. 'Are you ready?' I asked.

'Yes,' said Grace.

Carefully I untied the string• around the package. Then, together we pulled the sacks off. There wasn't a dead body inside. There was just a roll of cloth•. And we both recognized the cloth. It was from Salts Mill.

'They're stealing cloth from the mill,' I said shocked.

'We have to tell someone,' said Grace.

'Yes,' I said, 'but not yet. We'll come back tonight. We'll see who they meet.'

'I don't want to come back tonight,' said Grace.

'Then I'll come by myself,' I said. I wasn't afraid of the dark.

- **roll of cloth:** cylinder with cloth round it
- **slow coach:** expression to say someone is slow

- **string:**

When you worked in a mill, you were afraid of the machines and you were afraid of the overlooker. They were far more terrifying than the darkness. I loved the silence of night-time. And in fact, I loved the darkness because with the darkness came the end of the working day.

So that night, I walked back to the canal alone. It was a clear night and I could see the stars. I hid in some bushes near the cart, and waited. I didn't have to wait for long. First, the man with red hair came. He stood by the old cart and coughed, a horrible chesty cough• that broke the silence of the night. Then along came another man. I recognized him and my heart sank. It was Grace's father.

'Poor Grace,' I thought. 'I can't tell anyone about this. Grace's father will go to prison. The family will lose their house. Grace will lose her job. They'll have no money and no home. They'll die.'

I looked into the darkness for an answer. 'I have to tell someone,' I thought. And there was only one person I could tell. There was only one person I could trust. That was James. James' father was an important overlooker. 'The overlooker won't believe me. But maybe he'll believe his son. James loves me. He'll listen to me.'

The two men shook hands. Grace's father picked up the roll of cloth. 'I got five shillings for the last roll. That's a month's wages•. Here's your cut•.' He handed the red-haired man two shillings.

'Same time next week,' he called and then walked off into the night.

The red-haired man leant• against the old cart for a few minutes, coughing. Then he walked off in the opposite direction.

I waited a few minutes and then I ran home.

Glossary

- **chesty cough:** bad cough caused by mucus in the lungs
- **cut:** (here) part
- **leant:** put his body weight
- **wages:** salary

The next morning, the knocker-up• tapped• on the window and we all got up. It was 5.30 and it was still dark. We got dressed quickly and ran outside to join the stream• of workers going to the mill. We didn't have breakfast. There was a break for breakfast at 8.30.

As usual, Grace and I walked to the mill together. This was the one time in the day when we could chat.

'What happened?' asked Grace in an excited voice. 'Did you go?'

'Yes,' I said. 'They're stealing the cloth and selling it.'

'Really!' said Grace, shocked. 'I'm going to tell my father.'

'No, don't,' I said and I gripped Grace's wrist.

'Ouch! You're hurting me,' said Grace.

'Sorry,' I said. 'But you mustn't tell anyone, especially not your father.'

'But why not? That man's my father's friend,' said Grace.

'That's why you shouldn't tell him anything. It will upset him and you don't want to do that,' I said.

'No,' said Grace. Grace didn't want to upset her father. He was a wonderful father and she loved him. He wanted the best for his children. And even though he had no money, he always bought them little treats•.

The bell rang. It was 6 o'clock and the mill was open.

Emily

Do you think Emily does the right thing?
What would you do?

Glossary

- **knocker-up:** man whose job was to wake people so they could get to work on time (before alarm clocks)
- **stream:** (here) long, moving line
- **tapped:** made a noise
- **treats:** special, nice things

41

Caterina

A thought came to Jake and he stopped reading – Uncle Sanjit hadn't asked him what *he* wanted to do when he left school. No one asked him. They all just assumed that he wanted to be a basketball player. But he didn't. Yes, he was a good player and yes, he loved basketball but that wasn't the only thing he loved. Jake got off the bed and went to his desk. He pulled open the top drawer and took out a notepad and pen. He loved drawing. He didn't want to be a basketball player. He wanted to be an artist. I mean who was cooler: David Hockney or David Beckham? It was strange how most people his age thought that sport was cooler than art.

Jake wanted to go to art college. He was sure of that. He picked up the pen and started to draw. He drew the mill and he drew the girls leaving the mill, climbing the stone steps to Victoria Road above. One girl turned to face the reader. That was Emily. Only it wasn't Emily. Her face was familiar. It was Caterina's face. He was drawing Caterina.

'Where is Caterina, now?' he thought.

'What is she doing?'

He wanted to text her. Should he text her? Why not?

Message sent. No regrets.

Not yet anyway.

42

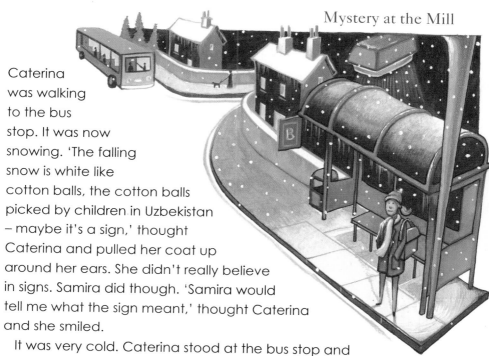

Caterina was walking to the bus stop. It was now snowing. 'The falling snow is white like cotton balls, the cotton balls picked by children in Uzbekistan – maybe it's a sign,' thought Caterina and pulled her coat up around her ears. She didn't really believe in signs. Samira did though. 'Samira would tell me what the sign meant,' thought Caterina and she smiled.

It was very cold. Caterina stood at the bus stop and waited. The snow was falling thick and fast now. The bus arrived and she got on. It moved off and slowly made its way into the town centre.

'Don't stay out too late,' said the bus driver as she got off. 'If it carries on snowing like this, there won't be any buses later.'

The snow was covering the ground so Caterina slid• down the street passed the Kirkgate Centre. Down past the Wool Exchange and across Market Street to where the old Brown & Muff department store had been until the late 1970s. This was Uncle Sanjit's new shop. Of course, it was different now but the building was the same.

Uncle Sanjit had explained to Jake and Caterina earlier that he used to come here as a child with his mother. All the other children looked at the toys, but Sanjit always looked at the clothes.

Glossary

• **slid:** (here) moved without walking because of the snow

Uncle Sanjit grew up in the 1970s, so the clothes he looked at in the window displays were stripey cat suits, purple flared trousers, platform shoes... At the time it was all so new and so colourful.

Back in the 1970s the LCD (Liquid Crystal Display) screen and floppy disk were invented. Skylab 3 carried the first fish and spiders into space. Abba had their first UK hit single with 'Waterloo'. The Bay City Rollers were pop idols, and Starsky and Hutch was a popular TV show. The film *Grease* was a box office hit at the cinema. Pink Floyd had a number one hit with 'Another Brick in the Wall', and the disco diva, Gloria Gaynor recorded her hit single 'I Will Survive'. Those were the 1970s and Uncle Sanjit had had a dream. He wanted to be a famous fashion designer.

1970s

What other things do you know about the 1970s?

Work in pairs.

Use the Internet to help you.

Then, Uncle Sanjit went to Saint Martins College in London to study fashion. Brown & Muff was closed down, too.

For years, the department store stood empty, a dusty building full of two centuries of memories. But every time Uncle Sanjit walked by, he imagined it filled with shoppers, admiring *his* designs. He imagined children stopping to stare at the wonderful window displays, and he imagined mothers finding just what they'd been looking for, for Britney or Jade, for Ali or Natasha or for Jamila or Abida. Brown & Muff had closed a long time ago but Caterina's mother often talked about it, too.

Caterina stood in front of it now, and she stared up at the new shop sign *Boho Chic*. Everybody was excited about the opening of this shop. *Be Chic on the Cheap. Look Cool for Next to Nothing.* The window displays were hidden behind brown paper. It had been like that for weeks. Everybody wanted to see what lay behind the plain brown paper.

45

Boho Chic

 Caterina saw a car park on the other side of the street.

'It must be Uncle Sanjit and the suppliers,' she thought. Quickly she turned to face the shop window. She listened to the voices that were muffled* by the snow and she heard the key turn in the lock. Then the voices faded to silence – just her and the snow now. She waited a few minutes. Then she went to try the door.

'Phew.* It's open,' she thought and slipped* inside.

It was dark, but there was a light on in a room at the far end of the shop. Caterina walked quietly towards it. She chose a clothes rail* near the office to hide behind. And from her hiding place, she could hear everything the men said. Their voices echoed loud and clear around the store.

'The cotton – why do you want to know where it was picked? Does it really matter?' asked Sid, one of the suppliers.

'Yes, it does,' said Uncle Sanjit. 'I don't want to use cotton picked by children. Now tell me where you bought the cotton or the deal's off*.'

'But you like our material. It's good quality and it's a good price,' said Aamir.

'Yes, yes, I know. But please tell me where you bought the cotton,' insisted Uncle Sanjit.

'India, of course,' said Sid suddenly. 'We always buy our cotton from a small cotton farm in India. We've visited it a few times and we can assure you that there are no children working there. The living conditions of the workers are very good. You're welcome to come and see for yourself. We can go there together if you like.'

Glossary

- **clothes rail:** metal construction on which clothes are hung
- **deal's off:** agreement is no longer valid
- **muffled:** made quieter
- **phew:** that's lucky
- **slipped:** (here) went quickly and silently

'Yes, one day I will come and visit the cotton fields with you,' said Uncle Sanjit. 'That's a relief•. I just need to know that the cotton isn't picked by children.'

'We understand,' said Sid. 'Now if that's all, I think you should go, Sanjit. It's snowing quite heavily out there.'

'Yes, you're right,' said Uncle Sanjit. 'Now here's the key to the flat• upstairs. I think you'll find everything you need up there. Oh and I'll leave the car here. I don't fancy• driving on a night like this. I'll walk, it's not far. I'll leave the car keys with you, just in case you need to move the car. We'll walk to the bank from here in the morning. I'll come for you about nine.'

'Okay, we'll see you first thing in the morning.'

'Good night then,' said Uncle Sanjit. Then Caterina watched as he left the shop.

'You lied to Sanjit,' said Aamir, the other supplier.

'So what?' said Sid. 'He's happy. We're happy. Everyone's happy. He doesn't need to know the cotton was picked in Uzbekistan.'

'Oh, no!' thought Caterina. 'Poor Uncle Sanjit. How dare• these men lie to him like that! What am I going to do now? I can't call the protest off now. The cotton most probably was picked by children.'

Ting ting went Caterina's phone. It was Jake's message. *Ting ting*, loud and clear – it echoed around the shop sounding like a fire alarm rather than a mobile phone. 'Oh no,' thought Caterina. 'Why didn't I switch my phone off?'

'What was that?' asked Aamir.

'It sounded like a mobile phone to me,' said Sid. 'There's someone in the shop.'

• **dare:** (here) can
• **fancy:** (here) want to
• **flat:** apartment

• **relief:** feeling of happiness after thinking something was bad

47

Sid ran out of the office. Caterina ran towards the main door but she wasn't fast enough. Sid threw himself at her legs and pulled her to the floor. Her head hit the floor. 'Ouch,' thought Caterina and that was her last thought before everything went black and the pain in her head stopped.

'We can't leave her here,' said Aamir in a panic. 'She's hurt.'

'We can't let her go,' said Sid. 'She heard everything. She'll tell Sanjit and he'll call the deal off. We need to keep her somewhere. Come on, Aamir. You're from round here. Where can we hide her?'

'Alright, alright. I'm thinking,' said Aamir. A clock ticked somewhere in the shop, tick, tick, tick, tick – the ticking made him nervous. He couldn't think straight. Tick, tick but then he remembered his uncle's old barge.

'I've got an idea,' said Aamir.

Trouble

 Jake continued reading the diary. He really wanted to know how Emily's story ended.

James and I wanted to get married. And then we wanted to run away – far away from the mill and the dust and the noise, the tiredness and the sore bones and the terrible coughs. We planned to find a small cottage, maybe in the Lake District. Someone told us it was pretty up there. We wanted to grow vegetables and keep sheep. I wanted to spin wool like my grandmother did. We wanted to send our children to school, so they could study hard, and not work and not grow up in a mill like us.

I told James about the cart and the roll of cloth and about Grace's father. He said he wanted to come and see for himself, so we agreed to meet that night, down by the canal.

There were no stars that night. I walked over the railway bridge. It had begun to snow heavily. I got to our meeting place but James wasn't there yet. The snow was falling thick and fast. 'I hope he comes soon,' I thought. I waited fifteen minutes but James didn't come.

I decided to go by myself. I didn't want to miss the men. I walked quickly along the canal, leaving my footprints in the fresh snow. When I came to the field, the men were already by the cart. I hid behind the bushes and then a terrible thing happened.

I tried to stop it but I couldn't. I waited until I could hardly breathe and then I coughed. The cough carried across the white field to the cart. The men turned their heads towards me. They knew that someone was watching them. Then the red-haired man was running towards me. I knew his name now. It was Tom. I knew I should run but I couldn't. I was frozen, frozen with cold or frozen with fear. Then the coughing continued. Tom was standing by me. He had six children. Janet the eldest worked with me.

'What are you doing here?' he asked. There was panic in his voice.

'You're stealing,' I said.

Grace's father was here now. 'Emily,' he said in a shocked voice. 'What are you doing here?'

'What do we do now?' asked Tom. 'We can't let her go back home. She'll tell everyone. We'll lose our jobs and our homes.'

'Does Grace know about this?' asked Grace's father.

I thought for a moment, then said quietly, 'Yes.'

Grace's father's face turned pale, pale as the snow falling around us. I felt sorry for him.

'She knows about the stealing, but she doesn't know it's you.'

'Thank God,' said Grace's father. 'Does anybody else know?'

I decided to lie: 'No,' I said. 'Just me and Grace. We went for a walk by the canal last week. We saw the barge stop and the men get off with the roll of cloth. We thought it was a dead body so we followed them to this cart.'

'She can't go home,' said Tom again. 'We'll tie her up and leave her on the barge for the night. We need to plan what to do.'

Emily and Caterina

Emily and Caterina are both in trouble
How are their situations similar?
How are they different?

🗩 Discuss in pairs.

'OK,' said Grace's father. I looked into his eyes and I knew he could never hurt me but I wasn't sure about Tom.

Quietly, I walked back to the canal with the two men. There was no point in trying to run away. My lungs were really bad that day and I was too weak.

It was still snowing and the canal was freezing over. They took me to a barge. Soon after we got to the barge, Grace's father left and went home. The other man, Tom, stayed to watch over me. I thought then that I was going to die.

I later learnt that James ran round to my house and banged loudly on the door. My father opened the door.

'Is Emily here?' James gasped•, out of breath.

'No, she isn't. She's at Grace's house,' said my father.

'Thanks,' said James and he ran off down the path. He knew I wasn't at Grace's house. He had just been there. He also knew that Grace's father wasn't there either. He knew I was in trouble. He had to go and find me. He ran over the railway bridge and down to the canal and then he saw something in the snow that looked like footprints. They were too small to be a man's.

'They could be Emily's,' thought James, and he decided to follow them. At first it was easy but the falling snow was covering everything fast. He followed them to the field and then there were lots of footprints, big and small. 'There's been a struggle•,' thought James, and he was really frightened now. He went over to the old cart and he saw the roll of cloth on the ground. 'Someone dropped this, and they left in a hurry,' he thought. 'Emily was right. Someone is stealing cloth from the mill.' This was all the evidence he needed. James looked around and then he followed what he thought were three sets of footprints back down to the canal. The branches on the trees above the towpath• were by now heavy with snow.

James ran as fast as he could through the silence and the snow. The only sound was his heart beating and his breath catching in his lungs.

Then suddenly he heard voices. He ran up the steep• path by the five locks• as best he could and then he saw me. I was wearing a blood red coat. My long black hair hung loose• around my shoulders.

The man pushed me and I screamed. The thin ice broke as I hit it and I was sucked• into its icy depths•.

'No,' screamed James, and he ran on up the path, slipping and sliding• in the snow. When James reached• the barge, he jumped into the canal but he knew he was too late. Nobody could survive this icy water.

As I sank deeper and deeper into the icy water, all my dreams sank with me. Yes, my dreams, for I had dreams, too. You know. I told you about them. But there's one more I haven't told you about. I was going to have a child and my child wasn't going to work in a mill. No, he was going to go to school and he was going to be a politician. He was going to save children like me. But now that wasn't going to happen. Down and down I went. Down into the icy blackness and down my dreams went too.

Guess

Do you think James will be able to save Emily?
Do you think Emily's dreams will sink with her in the canal?

🗣 Talk with a partner then share the class.

Glossary

- **depths:** deep parts
- **reached:** arrived at
- **slipping and sliding:** moving uncontrollably

- **sucked:** taken in quickly

The barge

When Caterina finally woke up, she felt cold and damp. There was a terrible pain in her head and a distinctive sound – the *put put put* of a canal barge. She was on the canal, but why? The last thing she remembered was going to see Jake. 'What happened after that? Think, girl, think!' Then she remembered and her heart started beating fast. 'The shop – Uncle Sanjit – the two men. Where are they taking me?' Then her imagination took over. 'They're going to throw me in the canal. It's all happening again. History is repeating itself. They're going to push me into the canal just like that man pushed my great-great grandmother,' thought Caterina. 'Perhaps this is the canal at Saltaire or is that too much of a coincidence? Samira wouldn't think so. Samira would say it's my destiny.'

Suddenly there was a very loud sound of fast moving water. 'Oh no! The barge is sinking.'

Caterina screamed but her scream could not compete with the sound of water. Water poured down on them, but the barge didn't sink, and then it clicked. 'Now, I know what's happening,' Caterina thought. 'It's OK. We're in a lock,' she thought and she breathed a sigh of relief. Then she had an idea. 'I'll count the locks. Then I'll know where we are.'

And so Caterina counted. 'Five locks! There's only one place in the whole country with five locks. I know where we are.' *Put put put*, the engine stopped and the barge came to a halt. She heard the men tie up the barge – then footsteps as they walked away. 'Are they coming back? How much time do I have to escape?' she wondered.

There was a chain around her left leg and it was locked to the door. She couldn't escape. Her hands were free but there was nothing she could do. Then, Caterina felt her phone in her pocket.

'If only I can text Jake. I can tell him where I am. He'll know what to do.' Quickly, she pulled the phone out of her pocket and went to messages.

Just then Caterina heard a voice and fear overcame her. The barge rocked as someone climbed on. Caterina panicked. 'I have to send it now,' she thought. Her hands trembled as she hit the send button. Hopefully Jake would understand where she was. She lay down on the floor again and shut her eyes. Now she could hear voices at the other end of the barge.

'Are you going to check on the girl?' said a voice.

'No. She's not going anywhere – not with that chain around her foot! Anyway, she's still unconscious. She hit her head really hard. What are we going to do with her anyway?'

'I don't know yet,' said Sid. 'We could sink the barge with her in it.'

'You're joking, right?' said Aamir, shocked.

'Maybe, maybe not!' said Sid smiling. 'But one thing's for sure, she's not going anywhere until Sanjit pays us for the material. And then, when we've got the money, we disappear back to London.'

'And leave her to a cold and watery death,' finished Aamir, scared.

'Who said anything about death? You watch too many horror films,' said Sid, slapping Aamir on the back.

'Please, Jake. Please, Jake. Please understand the message,' Caterina whispered over and over again to herself as she lay in the darkness.

No message from Caterina. Ten minutes later, still no message. Jake doodled* on his notepad. Half an hour, still no message. More doodling. 'Maybe she just doesn't want to answer my message.' More doodling. 'But what if something has happened? What could happen in the time it takes to walk from my house to Caterina's house?' Jake paced* the room now. 'What if she didn't go home? What if she followed my uncle?' An hour later ... Two hours later ...

Ting Ting Caterina's name flashed up on Jake's mobile and there was the message. 'I'm on the canal ... on a barge ... 5' ... 5 what? What can she mean? I've never been on the canal. I don't know what she means. Does she mean 5 bridges, 5 towns, 5 what? Jake needed help. Quickly he texted his best friend Simon:

'Meet me at the canal at Saltaire asap. Caterina's in trouble.' Simon didn't know Caterina. Jake deleted her name and put:

'I'm in trouble. Read this: I'm on the canal ... on a barge ... 5 ... Does the 5 mean anything to you? Tell me when we meet up.'

Ting Ting 'I'm on my way. 5? I'll have a think.'

The message smiled at him. Jake grabbed his coat and put the diary into his pocket. He didn't know why he was taking it. Maybe there was something in it that would help them find Caterina.

Once outside, he unchained his bike and got on it. It wasn't snowing any more, but the snow still lay thick on the ground. Jake pedalled as fast as he could through the silent white world. The number five went round and round his head.

Glossary

• **doodled:** drew pictures and designs   • **paced:** walked nervously around

When Jake got to Saltaire, Simon was standing on the railway bridge waiting for him. 'Five' – the mill was on the canal. Maybe Caterina meant five mill windows or five mill chimneys. Were there five mill chimneys? Jake didn't know. He braked hard and his bike skidded● down the slope, spraying snow everywhere until finally it came to a halt just in front of Simon.

'Impressive! What took you●?'

'We don't all have expensive bikes with twenty gears● and special snow tyres,' said Jake.

'Yeah, right. I wish.'

'So have you worked out what 'five' means?' asked Jake.

'Maybe. Have you?' asked Simon.

'No, but I think it's something to do with the mill. It's just a feeling,' said Jake, pushing his hands in his pockets and gripping the small leather book with his icy cold fingers.

'Well, I don't,' said Simon. 'There's only one five on the canal and that's the Five-rise Locks●.'

'Of course. That's where Caterina is,' said Jake.

'Caterina? Who's Caterina? And what's she got to do with all this?'

'Caterina?' said Jake. 'Umh … Caterina's the girl who's organizing the protest outside my uncle's shop on Saturday.'

'Oh, yeah. I remember,' said Simon. 'The girl who you ran off to see during basketball practice this afternoon.'

'Yes, her,' said Jake staring at the ground and kicking at the snow with his right foot.

'I still don't get it●,' said Simon.

'She's in trouble, not me. Now come on. She really is in trouble.'

Simon was about to tease● his friend but then he saw the scared look in his eyes.

Glossary

- **five-rise locks:** place with five locks together on a hill
- **gears:** (here) different speed settings
- **get it:** understand
- **skidded:** moved without control
- **tease:** laugh at
- **What took you?:** Why did you take so long?

'How far away are the five locks?' asked Jake.

'About ten or fifteen minutes if we pedal fast,' said Simon getting onto his bike. 'Come on. I'll race you there.'

It was hard pedalling along the snowy towpath but Jake was determined. He soon sped far ahead of* Simon. When he got to the five locks, he got off his bike and left it at the bottom of the steep slope. Up he ran, slipping and sliding in the snow. He could see an old barge tied at the top. Jake ran the last few metres as fast as he could. He was almost opposite the barge now. He looked over at it and saw Caterina's face pressed up against one of the windows. She saw him, too.

Glossary

* **sped far ahead of:** went much faster than

'There's nobody here,' she called. 'They've left me here.'
Jake saw the terror in her eyes and he saw her mouth opening and closing, but he couldn't hear her properly. He ran over the bridge to the other side of the canal and jumped onto the barge. Splash! Jake looked down in horror at the water around his feet.

'The barge is sinking,' he thought. Quickly, he found the room where Caterina was.

'It's sinking, we haven't got much time,' he said.

'I know,' said Caterina. 'They've left the key to the padlock in the kitchen. They told me. They didn't want to kill me. They just didn't want me to speak to your uncle.'

'Who?' asked Jake. 'Who did this?'

'Jake, we don't have time to talk now. I'll explain everything later. Go and find the key to this padlock and let's get off this barge before it sinks.'

'But they put a hole in the barge. They wanted you to die,' said Jake. 'They're murderers.'

'I don't think they put a hole in the barge. It just happened. It's old,' said Caterina. 'Now go and get the key.'

Jake went to the kitchen. The key was by the sink. It was easy to find. 'Maybe Caterina's right. Maybe they didn't want her to die,' thought Jake.

Quickly, Jake took the key and went back to unlock the padlock. The lock was old. Jake tried to unlock it but he couldn't. He looked down at the water. It was above his ankles now.

'The water's rising fast,' he thought, 'We've got to get out of here soon.'

• **murderers:** people who kill other
people

Simon was here now. 'Are you alright, Jake? Do you want some help down there?'

'No. Don't get on the barge. You'll only make it sink faster,' Jake shouted back anxiously. 'Call an ambulance.'

Jake's fingers were stiff and cold. He couldn't stop them from trembling. He was scared but he didn't want Caterina to know that. 'What if I can't unlock the padlock?' he thought. 'I can't leave Caterina on the barge by herself. I'll have to stay with her. We'll die together. Yeah, right. That's so not going to happen. Of course we'll get off the barge This isn't the *Titanic*, is it? And this isn't an ocean. It's the Leeds-Liverpool canal.' He turned the key one more time and the padlock came open.

'I've done it,' he said and he gave Caterina a hug. Then they both stared at each other embarrassed.

'Thanks,' she said quietly. 'I thought that was the end.' Suddenly the front of the barge sank forward. 'Come on. Let's get off before it's too late,' shouted Jake.

Simon was there on the towpath looking worried. He helped them climb off. Then they all stood and watched the barge sink as they waited for the ambulance.

Jake pushed his hands in his pockets. There was nothing there.

'The diary – I've lost the diary,' thought Jake. 'It was in my coat pocket but it's not there any more. Now I'll never know what happened to Emily. And how am I going to tell Caterina? She loves that diary.'

The ambulance finally arrived, sirens screaming and lights flashing. The paramedics• ran over to them and Jake forgot about the diary.

Glossary

- **paramedics:** (here) people who can give emergency medical care

Emily's Dream

It was a sunny Saturday morning. Caterina and her friends walked purposefully along the street to *Boho Chic*. They were all excited and a little nervous. They each had a handful of leaflets.

'So, we're really going to do this,' said Samira.

'Of course,' said Caterina. 'I've put too much work into it. I'm not going to back out now. You're not nervous, are you?'

'A bit,' said Samira. 'I've never done anything like this before.'

'It'll be alright,' said Caterina and linked arms with Samira.

They chatted happily as they walked along.

'Tell us again what happened that night,' begged Samira.

'And you say Jake rescued you. Wow! Lucky you!' said Helena.

Jake and Uncle Sanjit were standing on the steps of *Boho Chic* waiting for them. They'd taken down the brown paper from the shop windows and everyone could see the window displays.

'Wow! The shop looks amazing,' said Caterina.

'Thanks for coming along,' said Uncle Sanjit. 'And for writing the leaflets.'

'Jake helped me,' said Caterina. 'He did all the illustrations.'

'I know. He's good, isn't he?' Then he turned to face the others. 'Right. Everyone to their places now,' he said. 'And no chatting. You're here to work. You can all talk in the café later.'

'Yes readers, you've guessed. I've called the protest off. We're not here to hand out protest leaflets. We're here to hand out promotion leaflets for *Boho Chic*. But you still don't know the ending to Emily's story, do you? I'll tell you later. First let me bring you up-to-date on *Boho Chic*. Uncle Sanjit found some new suppliers who really do buy their cotton from a small farm in India. And guess what? He's promised to take me to visit the cotton farm in the summer holidays. Sid and Aamir's court case• is next month. I'm really nervous about that. I don't want to think about it now. Of course, the shop opening today is a huge success. Uncle Sanjit's designs are amazing. Well, so all my friends say, and I agree.'

After the shop closed, Caterina and Jake had a drink in the shop café. They were waiting for Uncle Sanjit and the staff• to finish cashing up•.

'Caterina, there's something I have to tell you,' said Jake.

Caterina looked up from her drink. Jake looked serious. 'What?' asked Caterina, worried.

Glossary

- **cashing up:** counting the money
- **court case:** legal process to judge if someone is guilty or innocent
- **staff:** people who work for a company

'That night when I rescued you from the canal barge, I had the diary with me and ...' he paused and looked at Caterina.

'And?' said Caterina.

'And I lost it,' said Jake miserably.

'Is that all?' asked Caterina, relieved.

'You mean you're not mad at me.'

'No. I typed the whole diary up on my laptop. So it's not lost.'

'Then can you tell me the end of the story? I didn't finish it and I really want to know what happened to Emily. Did she die?'

'She can't have died, can she? If she'd died, I wouldn't be here, would I, silly?' said Caterina and she laughed. Then she looked serious. 'Emily didn't die but she didn't get her fairy-tale ending.'

'Did she marry James?'

'Yes, she did but they never moved away to the Lake District. They stayed in Saltaire. She did have a son but he didn't go to university and he didn't become a politician. He worked in the mill.'

'So you must make her dream come true.'

'Yeah, very funny. I wish,' said Caterina.

After Reading
Personal Response

1 Did you like the story? Why/why not?

2 Could this story take place in your country? If not, why not?

3 Which part of the story did you enjoy most? Explain why.

4 What did you think of Caterina's ideas and actions? Would you do the same in her situation?

5 Is there anything you would like to change in the story? Give details.

6 What are the important messages in the story? Do you agree with them?

7 Did you like the ending of the story? Did you find it surprising? What did you think would happen?

8 Suggest other ways in which the story could end.

9 Have you ever read a story like this before?

10 Do you think this story would make a good film? Why/why not?

After Reading

Comprehension

Emily's story

1 Tick (✔) true (T) or false (F).

	T	F
a) Charles Dickens published *A Tale of Two Cities* in 1859.	☐	☐
b) Emily was Caterina's grandmother.	☐	☐
c) Emily and her friends worked in a clothes shop.	☐	☐
d) Grace's father was stealing cloth from the mill.	☐	☐
e) Emily was afraid of Grace's father.	☐	☐
f) Tom pushed Emily into the icy cold canal.	☐	☐
g) Emily drowned in the canal.	☐	☐

2 Correct the false sentences and write true sentences.

3 How many of these small details in the story did you notice? Complete the sentences.

a) In 1853, Emily's parents found work at the new .... mill outside Bradford.

b) Emily's family had a bigger house than the others because her father was an ....

c) Because of the dust Emily and her friends had difficulty ....

d) Emily thought there was a .... in the package that the two men hid under the cart.

e) Grace's father had no money but he always bought his children ....

f) James searched for Emily everywhere. Finally he saw some .... in the snow and he followed them.

g) James ran up the steep path by the .... Then he saw Emily.

70

Caterina's story

4 Number the events in the order they happened.

1	2	3	4	5	6	7	8	9	10
c									

a) Jake asked Caterina to call off the protest but she refused.

b) Caterina overheard the suppliers saying that they had lied to Uncle Sanjit: the cotton was picked in Uzbekistan.

c) Caterina found a little leather book with the story of Emily's life.

d) The suppliers kidnapped Caterina and left her on an old barge on the canal.

e) Caterina decided to protest about child labour outside Uncle Sanjit's new shop.

f) Caterina followed Uncle Sanjit to a meeting with his suppliers.

g) Jake learnt that Emily didn't drown in the canal and that she married James.

h) Everybody went to the opening of Uncle Sanjit's shop. It was a big success.

i) Jake rescued Caterina from the sinking barge.

j) Caterina fell and banged her head becoming unconscious.

5 Answer the questions with the name of a character from the story.

a) Whose grandfather came from India to work in the mills in England?

b) Who wants to go to the London School of Economics?

c) Who went to St Martins College to study fashion?

d) Who lied to Uncle Sanjit?

e) Whose uncle owned the old barge where they kept Caterina?

f) Who knows that the number five means the five locks?

g) Who found the key to unlock the padlock and rescue Caterina?

After Reading
Characters

1 Which characteristics do Emily and Caterina share? Tick the adjectives.

☐ determined   ☐ cautious   ☐ brave   ☐ cruel   ☐ ambitious

☐ kind   ☐ greedy   ☐ sensible   ☐ caring   ☐ selfish   ☐ impulsive

2 Work with a partner. Take it in turns to choose a character, describe him/ her to your partner using the adjectives below or any others you can think of. Your partner has to guess which character you are talking about.

Sid   Uncle Sanjit

Jake   Grace

ambitious   artistic   creative   dishonest   sad   sporty
superstitious   unethical   unlucky   violent

3 In pairs, discuss the characters' motives.

a) Grace's father was a good man. He loved his children. Why did he steal the cloth?

b) Why didn't Emily run away from the two men?

c) Why did Tom push Emily into the canal?

d) Caterina was organizing a protest outside Uncle Sanjit's new shop. Why was she organizing it? Why did Sanjit want to stop it?

e) Why did Sid and Aamir kidnap Caterina?

f) Jake asked Simon to meet him at the canal as soon as possible. Why?

4 Complete the paragraph about Emily with the words below.

eight years old   school   mill   children like her   easy
1851   great-great grandmother   Lake District

Emily was Caterina's **(a)** .... She was
born in **(b)** .... in Bradford, and she didn't
have an **(c)** .... life. She didn't go to
(d) .... Instead, she started working in
a mill when she was **(e)** .... She hated
working in the mill and she wanted to go and live
in a small cottage in the **(f)** .... If she
had a son, she wanted him to be a politician and save **(g)** ....
She got married and she had a son, but he didn't become a politician.
He worked in a **(h)** .... , too.

5 Match the sentences to the characters.

a) His father was an overlooker.

b) He guessed where
   Caterina was.

c) All the girls thought he was
   very good-looking.

d) He was Jake's best friend.

e) He loved Emily.

f) Caterina was frightened of him.

g) He supplied the cotton
   to Uncle Sanjit.

h) He wanted to study art.

Jake

James

Simon

Sid

**6 Choose one of the characters from Exercise 5.
Write a paragraph about him.**

After Reading
Plot and Theme

1 One of the main themes of the story is child labour. How much do you know about child labour? Do the quiz and find out. Then listen to check your answers.

a) Worldwide, ... million children work.

   1 □ 12   **2** □ 250   **3** □ 20   **4** □ 125

b) One in .... 5-14 year old children work in developing countries.

   1 □ two   **2** □ ten   **3** □ six   **4** □ five

c) School is important. Children of educated mothers are .... more likely to live beyond age 5.

   1 □ 40%   **2** □ 60%   **3** □ 20%   **4** □ 30%

d) .... million 15-24 year olds will not be able to read or write in 2015.

   1 □ 25   **2** □ 50   **3** □ 10   **4** □ 105

e) At the time of the 2002 World Cup, around .... children in Pakistan were employed making footballs for less than 70 cents a day.

   1 □ 1,000   **2** □ 15,000   **3** □ 5,000   **4** □ 10,000

2 Go back to Caterina's leaflet on pages **20** and **21**. In groups of three, discuss other types of child labour. Can you think of or find out about any charities or organisations which help to work against child labour.

Present your research to the class.

4 Which events happen in both stories? Read and tick (√).

a) ☐ There is a kidnapping.

b) ☐ A canal barge sinks.

c) ☐ Two men steal cloth from the mill.

d) ☐ A girl is rescued from the canal.

e) ☐ It snows.

f) ☐ Somebody tells a lie.

5 Put these events from Caterina and Emily's stories in the correct order.

Caterina

1	2	3	4	5

a) Caterina met Uncle Sanjit.

b) Caterina planned to protest at the opening of Uncle Sanjit's new shop.

c) Caterina and Jake wrote and designed a leaflet for the opening of *Boho Chic*.

d) Jake rescued Caterina from a sinking barge.

e) Caterina was kidnapped by Aamir and Sid.

Emily

1	2	3	4	5

a) The two men kidnapped Emily and pushed her into the canal.

b) Emily and her friend Grace discovered some men stealing cloth from the mill.

c) Emily's parents started working at Salts Mill.

d) Emily's boyfriend James dived into the canal to rescue her.

e) Emily discovered one of the men was Grace's father.

After Reading
Language

1 Which adjectives are used to describe the nouns below? Match and write.

icy	trendy	cheap	flared	polluted	chesty

a) .... scarves   b) .... cough

c) .... clothes   d) .... trousers

e) .... river   f) .... water

2 Complete the sentences with the noun and adjective pairs from the exercise above.

a) People wore .... in the 1970s.

b) The red-haired man had a terrible ....

c) No fish lived in the ....

d) She convinced him not to buy any more ....

e) Simon was very fashionable. He always wore ....

f) Nobody could swim in the .... It was too cold.

3 Match the everyday expressions from the story with their meanings.

a) □ Jump to it.
b) □ It's just a feeling.
c) □ You're joking, right?
d) □ I don't get it.
e) □ I know it means a lot to you.
f) □ My heart sank.

g) □ It costs next to nothing.

h) □ Don't jump to conclusions.
i) □ I don't fancy …
j) □ You're from round here.

1 I don't understand.
2 It's important to you.
3 I felt very sad.
4 You used to live in this area.
5 I don't want to …
6 You're not telling the truth, are you?
7 Find out all the facts before you decide something.
8 It's just an idea.
9 Do it now.
10 It's very cheap.

4 **Complete the sentences with the past simple or the past passive of the verbs below.**

| be | carry | write | open | record | publish | invent | start |

a) A *Tale of Two Cities* .... in 1859.

b) Big Ben .... ticking in 1859.

c) The Suez Canal .... in 1869.

d) Leo Tolstoy .... *War and Peace* in 1869.

e) The vacuum cleaner .... in 1869.

f) Skylab 3 .... the first fish into space in the 1970s.

g) 'I Will Survive' .... in the 1970s.

h) The film, *Grease* .... a box office hit in the 1970s.

5 **Find out about and then write sentences about the items below.**

Wuthering Heights   the iPhone   the laptop
Pride and Prejudice   the television

a) ....

b) ....

c) ....

d) ....

e) ....

6 **Choose a decade and write five sentences about it in your notebook.**

After Reading

Exit Test

P 1 **Read the story again and tick (✔) true (T) or false (F).**

	T	F
a) Dust from the mills gave lots of workers bad coughs.	☐	☐
b) The mills were quiet and safe places to work.	☐	☐
c) Jake and Caterina visted Salts Mill on a school trip.	☐	☐
d) Caterina was happy that her friends could buy trendy clothes cheaply.	☐	☐
e) Uncle Sanjit wasn't concerned about where his cotton came from.	☐	☐
f) Caterina went home after talking to Jake and Sanjit.		
g) Emily and her friends often went shopping at Brown & Muff.	☐	☐
h) Grace found out her father was stealing cloth from the mill.	☐	☐
i) Emily was discovered because of her cough and Caterina because of her phone.	☐	☐
j) Emily managed to persuade Grace's father to take her home.	☐	☐
k) Caterina didn't understand where she was on the barge.	☐	☐
l) Jake understood Caterina's text message straight away.	☐	☐
m) James found Emily because of the tracks in the snow.	☐	☐
n) Neither James nor Jake managed to save Emily or Caterina.	☐	☐
o) Caterina decided not to protest against Uncle Sanjit's new shop.	☐	☐

2 **Correct the false sentences.**

P 3 **Read and choose the correct answers.**

a) Emily is .... years old when she starts work at the mill.
1 ☐ six
2 ☐ eight
3 ☐ twelve
4 ☐ sixteen

b) The .... was invented in 1869.
1 ☐ TV
2 ☐ telephone
3 ☐ escalator
4 ☐ vacuum cleaner

c) In Bradford, ... percent of mill workers' children were dead by the age of fifteen.
1 ☐ ten
2 ☐ fifteen
3 ☐ twenty
4 ☐ thirty

d) Jake finds Caterina because she ....
1 ☐ sends him a text message
2 ☐ phones him
3 ☐ shouts and he hears her
4 ☐ leaves him a note

e) James finds Emily because ....
1 ☐ Grace's father tells him where she is
2 ☐ she sends him a text message
3 ☐ Grace helps him
4 ☐ he sees her footprints in the snow

f) In the end, Emily ....
1 ☐ moves to the Lake District
2 ☐ marries James and continues working in the mill
3 ☐ drowns in the canal
4 ☐ becomes a politician

P 4 **In pairs, choose two different pictures in the book. Take turns telling each other what you can see in your picture.**

After Reading

Projects

WEB 1 **Find out about Fairtrade.**

What is Fairtrade?
Fairtrade makes sure that:

- farmers earn enough money to support their families and have a better future.
- farmers and workers have safe and healthy working conditions through fairer trading conditions, fair prices and a premium (extra money).
- child labour is not permitted and immediate action is always taken to stop this when it happens.
- the natural environment is protected by:

 reducing the amount of chemicals used

 saving water

 producing less waste

2 **Listen to the story of a group of Fairtrade cocoa farmers. Write a short text about them including the words in the box below.**

| West Africa   chocolate bar   afford   earn   *Divine*   shares |
| charity   Comic Relief   wrapper   competition |